A Cozy Book of
Tea Time Treats

A Cozy Book of Tea Time Treats

40 Bite-Size Desserts to Sweeten Your Day

Beth Allen

Prima Publishing

PRIMA PUBLISHING and colophon are registered trademarks of Prima Communications, Inc.

Library of Congress Cataloging-in-Publication Data

Allen, Beth
    A cozy book of tea time treats : 40 bite-size desserts to sweeten your day / Beth Allen.
    Previously published under the title Life's little temptations.
      p.   cm.
    Includes index.
    ISBN 0-7615-0871-6
    1. Desserts   2. Cakes   I. Title
    TX773.A357   1994
    641.8′6—dc20   94-21796
                                                    CIP

96 97 98 99 00 01 AA 10 9 8 7 6 5 4 3 2 1
Printed in the United States of America.

How to Order

Single copies may be ordered from Prima Publishing, P.O. Box 1260BK, Rocklin, CA 95677; telephone (916) 632-4400. Quantity discounts are also available. On your letterhead, include information concerning the intended use of the books and the number of books you wish to purchase.

Visit us online at http://www.primapublishing.com

To my husband, John,

who never outgrows his enthusiasm

for tasting my latest recipe creation!

Acknowledgments

A great big sweet thanks to all those who helped me create this book of little sweet temptations: my family and friends for always being ready to try the next recipe; Michelle Gurdon for her help with baking, recipe testing, and tasting; David Schoen for his computer knowledge and patience; my indexer, Catherine Dorsey, for her superb cross-referencing abilities; my agent, Sheree Bykofsky, for all of her guidance and advice; and, most of all, the folks at Prima Publishing, especially my editor, Jennifer Basye Sander, for making *A Cozy Book of Tea Time Treats* a reality!

Contents

Sweet Samplings   xiii

Happy moments often mean sweet moments . . .
so go ahead and enjoy the delicious ones here.
By baking them in small sizes, you cut back
on the fat and calories you eat,
while still enjoying each scrumptious bite!

Petite Techniques   xv

A few tips, tricks, and techniques for making, shaping, and baking
little temptations—simply and easily, time after time

Brunch Bites   1

Small sweet-somethings to start your day—for breakfast, brunch, or in between

A Taste of Cake   14

*Those old-fashioned cakes baked into little bite-size tastes for enjoying
at tea time, dessert time, anytime*

Dots of Cookies   30

*Little tempting cookies to fill your cookie jar—from small balls
of cookies to tiny thumbprints and stars*

Baby-Bar Cookies   44

Some of those old-fashioned pan cookies, baked all at once,
then cut into tiny bars of heavenly bites

Banana Crunch Bars   46
Mini Marble Bars   48
Double-Date Bars   50
Lemon Lites   52

Tiny Tarts   54

Petite pies, filled with cremes, custards, and fruits,
then decorated party-perfect

Tiny Buttery Crusts   56
Raspberry Petite Pies   58
Strawberry Tiny Tarts   60
Lemon Cremes   62

Petite Pickin's   64

Mini puffs of pastries and small pieces of fruit and cheese bites for sweet tastings

Fruit Boats   66
Raspberry Cream Puffs   68
Petite Eclairs   70
Orange Marnier Crêpes   72

Visions of Sugarplums   74

Small sweet-somethings, which scrumptious memories are made of

Chocolate Kisses   80

*Tiny kisses of chocolate creations to tempt you and your friends,
any time of day*

Index   91

Sweet Samplings

Happy moments often mean sweet moments . . .

Throughout the years, the sweet moments are the ones that bring back some of my happiest memories. Sweet moments like my father's annual Fourth-of-July barbecues, when Mom always made her Southern shortcakes of buttery biscuits, then smothered them with fresh strawberries and rich spoon cream . . .

Sweet moments, too, like our holiday baking sessions when the whole family cut out sugar cookies, decorated them with colored sugars, then hung them carefully on the tree with bright red bows.

But perhaps the sweetest moments of them all were my birthday parties. The highlight was Mom's homemade cakes, which always looked a mile high to me when I was standing on my tiptoes blowing out the candles! My cake, by special request, was always angel food, swirled with pink frosting and showered with fresh coconut.

But somewhere along the way, in the midst of all of the recent awareness of good, healthful eating, such sweet moments have made us feel just a little guilty, especially when we succumb to our temptations and have more than one piece of cake or a few too many cookies. So gradually, the word *moderation* has become the sensible, smart way to eat—especially when we are considering "something sweet."

---

*Go ahead . . . indulge in those tempting, scrumptious sweets—
but in petite sizes, please!*

Moderation, in other words, *less is better,* makes good, sound sense, especially with sweets. So get ready to treat yourself to some of these heavenly homemade sweets in the pages that follow (there are even small angel cups based on my birthday cakes!). And pull out some of those family favorite recipes too, such as your grandmother's fudge cake that you probably haven't made for years.

Just remember to "think small!" Forget about serving oversized, double-decker slices of cake. Bake the same batter in a single layer, and cut up tiny tastes of cake instead. In place of baking double-crust, deep-dish pies, make tiny tarts, with only a bottom crust and lots of fresh berries on top. Cut baby bars of cookies instead of giant ones . . . spoon muffin batter into mini-muffin pans . . . bake up small dots of cookies . . . shape candies into tiny bites.

These recipes use the best of ingredients—butter, eggs, fresh fruits, whole milk, and even some heavy cream—but in moderation of course. We've used just enough to capture all those homemade flavors that sweet memories are made of. Plus, we've used as few ingredients as possible and simple techniques that make these recipes easy and fun to make. Then, we've shaped, baked, cut, and sliced them into small sizes—giving you fewer calories and fat in each cookie, every piece of candy, or each taste of cake.

Start right now to discover the scrumptious memories that
A Cozy Book of Tea Time Treats *is made of!*

Petite Techniques

While creating the recipes tucked inside these pages, we discovered a few tricks, tips, and techniques that make the mixing, shaping, and baking of *A Cozy Book of Tea Time Treats* easier and more reliable, time after time. Master these few procedures and you're on your way to enjoying scrumptious sweets, while still keeping the fats and calories in control, at the same time.

Select sweets that can easily be made in small sizes.

Choose sweets such as bar cookies that cut easily into baby bars . . . breads such as muffins that bake quickly in mini pans . . . desserts such as fruit pies that bake into tiny tarts . . . cake batters that bake into tiny cupcakes.

Find some petite pans.

In keeping with the current trend of eating less, equipment manufacturers are designing petite-size pans. Look for them in specialty cook shops or cook's catalogs:

- *Mini-muffin tins*   These usually come 24 mini-muffin cups to each pan, with each cup 2 inches wide, 1 inch deep. For easy cleaning, look for the nonstick ones. **Baker's Tip:** By lining the cups with mini paper liners, which stand up higher than the pan, you can spoon a little more batter into each cup and bake higher mini muffins!

- *Mini-tart pans*   These individual mini-tart pans with slanted *fluted* sides make very fancy-looking tarts. Naturally, mini-muffin tins with slanted straight sides make nice tiny tarts too.

- *Little loaf pans*   These come in two sizes: one that makes six loaves about 3 ³/₄ by 2 ¹/₂ inches. The other pan, often used by the fancier restaurants, makes four dinner-size loaves, about 5 ¹/₂ by 3 inches. Both pans come with nonstick finishes, for easy care.

- *Madeleines*   These pans with their shallow shell-shaped patterns are perfect for baking oblong fluted sponge-cake-like cookies, about 3 inches long and 2 inches wide. Small 2-inch shell-shaped madeleine pans are available too.

- *Popover pans*   Six individual popover cups are banded together in each set, each cup about 2 ¹/₂ inches wide and 2 ¹/₄ inches deep. These are ideal for baking individual petite angel food cakes, about 3 inches wide, 4 inches deep. Try baking our Angel Cups on page 16.

Master the art of using a pastry bag.

Many petite sweets can quickly (and oh so easily!) be piped into mini-bites, such as the Raspberry Cream Puffs on page 68 and the Petite Eclairs on page 70. Once you've discovered how simple a pastry bag is to use, you'll find many other tricks with it too, such as piping ice cream into rosettes. Be sure to pop them back into the freezer to freeze solid! These same bags are great for piping butter cookie dough into fancy small shapes too.

Be on the lookout for small cookie cutters.

Small is in these days, especially in cookie cutters! Look for small hearts for Valentine's Day, mini gingerbread people and petite stars for Christmastime, little leaves for decorating tiny tarts, small round fluted cutters for tiny biscuits and scones. One of my treasures that I own is a set of canapé and hors d'oeuvre cutters that are ideal for cutting sliced bread for tiny sandwiches, rolled-cookie dough for petite sweets, and biscuit dough into tiny fabulous shapes such as cloverleaves, diamonds, and spades.

When baking cakes, think thin.

Instead of pouring the batter for a two-layer cake into large round pans, spread it into a jelly-roll pan (15 1/2 by 10 1/2 by 2 inches) instead. Bake for about one-third less time than the recipe calls for, then remove the cake from the oven when a toothpick inserted in the center comes out with a moist crumb. Let it cool, then cut into thin fingers of cake. Check out our Frosted Fudge Fingers on page 28!

Spread the frosting sparingly!

A thin layer of frosting, instead of a thick fluffy one, cuts down on the sweetness, and the calories too. Yet it still gives that *little sweet something* in every bite.

Shop smartly—with small in mind!

Look for ingredients that come in petite pieces, such as mini chocolate chips, tiny flakes of coconut, mini marshmallows, and small raspberries, instead of larger berries like strawberries or blackberries. Their smaller size bakes up better in tiny cakes, cookies, and muffins.

Chop, slice, grate, and dice in small shapes.

When you are making baby-bar cookies, chop the nuts extra-fine. (They cut easier in little bars, this way!) When making the Carrot Cake Cups on page 26, we've cooked and puréed the carrots to make batter that bakes easily into tiny cakes.

Store petite sweets with extra care.

Small sweets, especially tiny tastes of cakes and baby-bar cookies, need careful wrapping and airtight containers to keep them fresh. Store them only in airtight cookie jars. When freezing them, wrap two or three pieces in plastic wrap, then tuck them in freezer-lock bags in the coldest part of the freezer.

Brunch Bites

Come for brunch . . . or just a
spur-of-the-moment coffee klatch.

Whatever the reason or season, you will soon discover, if you haven't already, that brunch is a fun and informal way to entertain. And it's the perfect time to mix up a few sweet little temptations. Bake up a batch of buttery bites of biscuits, stuffed with tiny bits of baked ham or small sausage balls . . . let your guests help flip up some petite pancakes sprinkled with fresh berries . . . cook up bite-size doughnuts tied in matrimony love knots. All are small, just sweet enough, and scrumptious—the perfect way to round out a brunch, a coffee klatch, and even teatime too.

Berry Patch Petite Pancakes

The next time you see fresh blueberries or raspberries in the market, buy them and stir up some of these petite pancakes for breakfast. They're the size of silver dollars and have just a hint of sweetness that complements the fresh berries.

1 ¹/₃ cups all-purpose flour	6 tablespoons (³/₄ stick) unsalted
¹/₄ cup granulated sugar	butter (not margarine), melted
1 tablespoon baking powder	1 tablespoon vanilla extract
1 teaspoon salt	1 cup fresh raspberries or blue-
1 ¹/₃ cups whole milk	berries, stemmed and washed
1 large egg	Vegetable oil

1. In a medium-size bowl, mix the flour, sugar, baking powder, and salt. In a small bowl, whisk together the milk, egg, butter, and vanilla.
2. Pour the milk mixture into the center of the flour mixture, all at once. Whisk the batter just until smooth, then gently fold in the berries.
3. Heat a nonstick griddle or large skillet over medium-high heat and brush with a little vegetable oil. Using a rounded tablespoon of batter for each cake, spoon the batter onto the griddle, about 2 inches apart.
4. Cook the cakes for about 3 minutes or just until they are covered with bubbles. Flip them over and cook 2 minutes more or until golden-brown. Serve immediately with warm maple syrup.

Makes about 2 ¹/₂ dozen petite pancakes.

Banana-Berry Muffins

Almost everyone has a favorite banana bread . . . this one is mine. I created it one summery day when I had extra-ripe bananas and fresh strawberries on hand. The same batter that bakes into a perfect loaf of bread makes marvelous mini muffins!

2	cups all-purpose flour
1	tablespoon baking powder
1/2	teaspoon baking soda
1/2	teaspoon salt
1/2	cup (1 stick) unsalted butter (not margarine), at room temperature
1	cup firmly packed light brown sugar
2	large eggs
1	cup mashed ripe bananas (about 3 medium)

1	cup finely chopped fresh ripe strawberries
1	cup finely chopped walnuts, toasted
3/4	cup white corn syrup, warmed (optional)
1	pint fresh strawberries, washed, hulled, and sliced lengthwise (optional)

1. Preheat the oven to 350°F. Line 24 mini-muffin cups (2 inches in diameter, 1 inch deep) with paper liners. Onto a piece of wax paper, sift the flour, baking powder, baking soda, and salt.

2. In a large bowl, beat the butter until creamy, using an electric mixer on high. Gradually add the sugar, then the eggs, one at a time, and continue beating for 3 minutes until light yellow and fluffy.

3. Using a wooden spoon, stir half of the flour mixture into the butter mixture. Blend in the bananas, then stir in the remaining flour. Fold in the chopped strawberries and walnuts, then fill the muffin cups with the batter until almost full.

4. Bake for 15 minutes or until golden brown. Let the muffins stand in the pans on racks for 5 minutes before removing. Garnish if you wish, by brushing the top of each muffin with the warmed corn syrup and arranging a strawberry slice in the center.

Baker's Tip: For a heavenly bread, preheat the oven to 350°F. Butter a 9 × 5 × 3-inch loaf pan and line the bottom with wax paper. Make 1 recipe of batter for Banana-Berry Muffins, spoon into the pan, and bake for 1 hour or until a cake tester inserted in the center comes out with moist crumbs. Cool the bread in the pan on a rack for 20 minutes before removing.

Makes 2 dozen mini muffins or one 9 × 5 × 3-inch loaf of bread.

Buttery Biscuit Bites

Hot bread every night is an old Southern custom that was religiously followed in our Texas home. And biscuits were always what I liked best—and still do. These are small, buttery, and flavored with just a hint of lemon. For brunch, try stuffing them with small bites of ham and a little honey!

2 cups sifted all-purpose flour	1/2 cup (1 stick) cold unsalted
1 tablespoon baking powder	butter (not margarine), cut into
3/4 teaspoon salt	16 cubes
2 teaspoons grated lemon peel	3/4 cup half-and-half

1. Preheat the oven to 450°F and butter 2 baking sheets. In a large bowl, sift the flour, baking powder, and salt, then stir in the lemon peel.
2. Using a pastry cutter or 2 knives, cut in the butter until the mixture resembles coarse crumbs. Pour in the half-and-half, all at once. Using a wooden spoon, mix just until the flour disappears and a soft dough forms.
3. Turn out the dough onto a lightly floured board. Knead lightly for about 30 seconds, then pat the dough into a circle, 3/4-inch thick.
4. Using a 1 3/4-inch floured biscuit cutter (a fluted one is especially nice), cut out the dough into rounds, re-rolling the scraps of dough as you go. (You should have about 30.) For flaky tender biscuits, avoid adding extra flour or overworking the dough. Place the biscuits 1 inch apart on the baking sheets and brush the tops with a little extra half-and-half, if you wish.
5. Bake for 8 to 10 minutes or just until puffy and golden. For biscuits with soft tops, brush the tops of the biscuits with a little melted butter as soon as they come out of the oven. Serve piping hot!

Makes about 2 1/2 dozen biscuit bites.

Orange Swirls

To my favorite sweet yeast dough I've added a hint of fresh oranges, then shaped the dough into small swirls and rolled them up with a spicy pecan filling. They bake into that perfect sweet-something for brunch—and are a terrific teatime treat too.

Dough

1/3	cup lukewarm water (105° to 110°F)
1	packet (1/4 ounce) active dry yeast
6	tablespoons granulated sugar
1	cup whole milk
1/2	cup (1 stick) unsalted butter (not margarine)
1	teaspoon salt
1	large egg, well beaten
2	teaspoons grated orange peel
4 1/2	cups all-purpose flour
1/4	cup fresh orange juice

Orange Filling

1 1/2	cups finely chopped pecans (not toasted)
3/4	cup firmly packed light brown sugar
3/4	cup granulated sugar
4	teaspoons grated orange peel
2	teaspoons ground cinnamon
1/4	cup (1/2 stick) unsalted butter (not margarine), melted

Creamy Icing

1 1/2	cups sifted confectioners' sugar
3	tablespoons heavy cream
1/2	teaspoon grated orange peel

1. *To make the Dough:* Pour the water into a large bowl, then stir in the yeast and 2 tablespoons of the sugar; let stand for 5 minutes or until creamy and foamy.

2. Meanwhile, in a medium-size saucepan, heat the milk, butter, the remaining 4 tablespoons of sugar, and the salt, just until bubbles start to form. Cool to luke-warm, then stir into the yeast mixture, along with the egg and orange peel.

3. Stir in 1 cup of the flour, then the orange juice, then the remaining 3 1/2 cups of flour. Beat until a soft dough forms, then transfer to a lightly floured surface. Knead the dough for 8 minutes or until smooth and elastic.

4. Transfer to a large buttered bowl and turn the dough over, coating it with the butter. Cover loosely with a clean towel and let rise in a warm place for 1 hour or until the dough has doubled in size. Butter 2 baking sheets.

5. *While the dough rises, make the Orange Filling:* In a medium-size bowl, toss the pecans with both of the sugars, the orange peel, and the cinnamon.

6. Punch down the dough and knead on a lightly floured surface for 1 minute. Halve the dough and roll out 1 piece into an 18 × 14-inch rectangle about ³/₈-inch thick. Brush the dough with one-half of the melted butter and sprinkle with one-half of the filling. Starting at one wide end, roll up jelly-roll fashion. Cut into 1-inch-thick slices and place cut-side-up on baking sheets. Repeat with the remaining piece of dough. (You should have about 36 rolls.) Preheat the oven to 375°F and let the rolls rise for 30 minutes. Bake for 15 minutes or just until light brown.

7. *While the rolls bake, make the Creamy Icing:* In a medium-size bowl, stir together all of the icing ingredients until well blended. Pour into a pitcher, then drizzle over the warm rolls.

Makes about 3 dozen petite frosted sweet rolls.

Sugary Orange Scones

In England, scones are often simple and plain, just waiting for fresh strawberry preserves and rich Devonshire clotted cream. These scones are more buttery and sugary than the ones I have enjoyed in England, with a fragrance of fresh orange and a hint of spice that are hard to resist.

2   cups all-purpose flour
1/3 cup + 3 tablespoons granulated sugar
1   tablespoon baking powder
1   teaspoon salt
1/4 teaspoon ground nutmeg

1   tablespoon grated orange peel
1/2 cup (1 stick) cold unsalted butter (not margarine), cut into 16 cubes
3/4 cup heavy cream
1   large egg

1. Preheat the oven to 425°F and butter 2 baking sheets. In a large bowl, mix the flour with the 1/3 cup of sugar, the baking powder, salt, and nutmeg, then toss with the orange peel.

2. Using a pastry cutter or 2 knives, cut in the butter until the mixture resembles coarse crumbs. In a small bowl, whisk together the cream and egg until frothy then pour into the center of the flour mixture, all at once. Using a wooden spoon, mix just until the flour disappears and a soft dough forms.

3. Turn out the dough onto a lightly floured surface. Knead lightly for about 30 seconds, then pat the dough into a circle, 3/4-inch thick.

4. Using a 1 3/4-inch floured pastry cutter (a fluted one is especially nice), cut out the dough into rounds, re-rolling the scraps of dough as you go. (You should have about 30.) Place the scones 1 inch apart on the baking sheets and sprinkle the tops with the remaining 3 tablespoons of sugar.

5. Bake the scones for 8 minutes or just until puffy and golden. Serve hot with sweet orange marmalade or sweetened whipped cream.

Makes about 2 1/2 dozen petite scones.

Cinnamon Crullers

The New Amsterdam Dutch settlers introduced us to these egg-rich fried pastries called crullers (from the Dutch word *krullen*). Often crullers are cut into strips, then twisted before cooking; other times they are tied into love knots or matrimony knots.

3 1/2 cups sifted all-purpose flour
1 tablespoon baking powder
3/4 teaspoon salt
1 teaspoon ground cinnamon
4 large eggs
1 1/2 cups granulated sugar

6 tablespoons (3/4 stick) unsalted butter (not margarine), melted
1 teaspoon grated lemon peel
1/3 cup whole milk
Vegetable oil for frying

1. Onto a piece of wax paper, sift the flour with the baking powder, salt, and 1/2 teaspoon of the cinnamon. In a large bowl, with an electric mixer on high, beat the eggs until thick and lemon colored. Gradually beat in 1 cup of the sugar, 1/4 cup at a time, then blend in the butter and lemon peel.
2. Stir in the flour mixture, alternating with the milk, one-third at a time, beginning and ending with the flour. Divide the dough into 2 equal pieces, wrap in plastic wrap, and refrigerate for 30 minutes.
3. In a deep skillet, preheat about 2 inches of oil to 375°F. On a lightly floured surface, roll out 1 piece of the dough, 1/4-inch thick. Cut with a fluted pastry wheel into 3 × 1-inch strips. Twist each strip about 4 times, then slide it gently into the hot oil.

4. Cook the crullers for about 2 minutes on each side or until light brown. Using a slotted spoon, transfer to paper towels to drain. On a plate, mix the remaining $1/2$ cup of sugar with the $1/2$ teaspoon of cinnamon. Roll the warm crullers in the spiced sugar until lightly coated.

Baker's Tip: For love knots, cut the dough into 5 × 1-inch strips, $1/4$-inch thick. Tie each strip into a knot and cook in the hot oil for about 3 minutes on each side. Roll in the cinnamon-sugar as for the crullers.

Makes about 4 dozen crullers or 2 $1/2$ dozen love knots.

A Taste of Cake

Cakes are not only for birthdays—
but other days in between too!

_S_weet cake temptations are too scrumptious to save just for birthdays. They're perfect for many other occasions too—dessert time, teatime, snack time, anytime. We've taken many of our old-fashioned favorites, like lemony angel food and carrot cake, kept in all of the tempting flavors, then baked them in small, bite-size portions, so you can enjoy them often. There are tiny balls of coconut cream cakes, heavenly bites of cheesecake, and fresh blueberry jam cakes. And naturally there's a dark fudge cake, which we've cut into thin fingers. They're tiny taste treats you'll bake again and again!

Angel Cups

My favorite birthday cake was (and still is!) angel food cake. This batter bakes in small popover cups to give the same taste treat, but just less of it. If you're cutting back on fat, forget the glaze and simply dust the cakes with a little confectioners' sugar.

Angel Cakes

3/4	cup sifted cake flour
1	cup granulated sugar
8	large egg whites (1 cup)
1	teaspoon cream of tartar
1/4	teaspoon salt
2	teaspoons vanilla extract
1/2	teaspoon almond extract

Creamy Glaze

6	tablespoons (3/4 stick) unsalted butter (not margarine)
2	cups sifted confectioners' sugar
3	tablespoons fresh lemon or orange juice
1	teaspoon grated lemon or orange peel

1. *To make the Angel Cakes:* Preheat the oven to 350°F and set out 12 regular-size non-stick popover cups (do not butter them). Onto a piece of wax paper, sift the flour with 1/4 cup of the granulated sugar.

2. In another large bowl, with an electric mixer on medium, beat the egg whites, cream of tartar, and salt until frothy. Increase the speed to high and beat until soft peaks form. Gradually beat in the remaining 3/4 cup of granulated sugar, one-third at a time, then the vanilla and almond extracts, and continue beating until the egg whites stand in stiff glossy peaks.

3. Sift the flour mixture, one-third at a time, over the egg white mixture and gently fold it in, just until the flour disappears. Spoon the batter into the popover cups and bake for 15 minutes or until golden and dry on top. Let the cakes cool completely in the pans on a rack before removing. Place a rack on a baking sheet, turn the cakes out on the rack, then drizzle the tops with the Creamy Glaze.

4. *While the cakes bake, make the Creamy Glaze:* In a small saucepan, melt the butter over medium heat. In a medium-size bowl, place the sugar, then stir in the hot butter. Add the juice and peel and stir until smooth. Drizzle over the tops of the cooled cakes.

Makes 1 dozen frosted angel cups.

Coconut Snowballs

As one of my friends recently exclaimed: "These cakes are how to make a birthday great!" They're really for coconut lovers, as they have coconut in the cake, as well as on top.

Snowballs

2	cups sifted cake flour
2	teaspoons baking powder
3/4	teaspoon salt
3/4	cup (1 1/2 sticks) unsalted butter (not margarine), at room temperature
1 1/2	cups granulated sugar
4	large eggs, separated
2	teaspoons coconut extract
1	teaspoon vanilla extract
1	cup light cream
2	cups flaked coconut, divided

Lemon Cream Frosting

1	package (8 ounces) cream cheese at room temperature
4 1/2	cups sifted confectioners' sugar (one 1-pound box)
1/4	teaspoon salt
2	to 3 tablespoons light cream
2	teaspoons grated lemon peel

1. *To make the Snowballs:* Preheat the oven to 350°F. Line 48 mini-muffin cups (2 inches in diameter, 1 inch deep) with paper liners. Onto a piece of wax paper, sift the flour, baking powder, and salt.

2. In a large bowl, with an electric mixer on high, cream the butter with 1 cup of the granulated sugar until light yellow. Beat in the egg yolks and both of the extracts and continue beating 3 minutes more or until thick and lemon colored.

3. Using a wooden spoon, stir in the flour mixture, one-third at a time, alternating with the cream, beginning and ending with the flour. Fold in 1 cup of the coconut.

4. In a clean medium-size bowl, with an electric mixer on high, beat the egg whites with clean beaters until frothy. Gradually beat in the remaining $1/2$ cup of granulated sugar until stiff peaks form. Using a wire whisk, gently fold the beaten whites into the batter.

5. Spoon the batter into the muffin cups until three-fourths full and bake for 15 minutes or until a cake tester inserted in the center comes out with moist crumbs. Let the cakes stand in the pans on racks for 5 minutes, then turn out onto the racks to cool. After the cakes have cooled completely, frost with the Lemon Cream Frosting.

6. *To make the Lemon Cream Frosting:* In a medium-size bowl, with an electric mixer on high, beat the cream cheese until smooth and fluffy. Stir in the remaining ingredients, then continue beating 3 minutes more or until light and creamy. Swirl the frosting on the top of the cakes, sprinkling with the remaining cup of coconut as you go. Refrigerate until serving time.

Baker's Tip: This recipe also bakes perfectly into one 9-inch two-layer cake. Preheat the oven to 350°F. Butter and flour two 9-inch round layer cake pans and line the bottoms with wax paper. Make one recipe of the batter for Coconut Snowballs and divide between the 2 pans. Bake for 25 to 30 minutes or until a cake tester inserted in the center comes out with moist crumbs. Let the cakes cool in the pans on a rack for 5 minutes, then turn out onto the rack to cool. Make one recipe of the Lemon Cream Frosting and spread between the cooled layers, on the sides, and on top, sprinkling with the remaining cup of coconut as you go.

Makes 4 dozen mini snowballs or one 9-inch two-layer cake.

Lemon Tea Cakes

Thumbing through my grandmother's recipe treasures, I found a heavenly recipe for her feathery lemon cake, which I have used as a basis for creating these tiny tea cakes. They are so delicate that only a light dusting of powdered sugar and perhaps a fresh raspberry are needed for that finishing touch. No frosting's required! I love to serve these petite cakes with steaming orange and spice tea. Pour the tea into your fanciest cups, then add a cinnamon stick "stirrer" in each.

1 1/2 cups sifted cake flour	1/3 cup fresh lemon juice
1 teaspoon baking powder	1 tablespoon grated lemon peel
1/4 teaspoon + pinch of salt	Sifted confectioners' sugar
1/2 cup (1 stick) unsalted butter (not margarine), at room temperature	1/2 pint fresh raspberries (about 1 cup)
1 cup granulated sugar	
3 large eggs, separated	

1. Preheat the oven to 350°F. Line 30 mini-muffin cups (2 inches in diameter, 1 inch deep) with paper liners. Onto a piece of wax paper, sift the flour with the baking powder and the 1/4 teaspoon of salt.

2. In a large bowl, with an electric mixer on high, cream the butter with the granulated sugar until light yellow. Beat in the egg yolks, one at a time, and continue beating 3 minutes more or until thick and lemon colored. Using a wooden spoon, stir in the flour mixture, one-third at a time, alternating with the lemon juice, beginning and ending with the flour. Add the lemon peel.

3. In a clean bowl, beat the egg whites and the pinch of salt with clean beaters on high until stiff peaks form. Gently fold into the butter-flour mixture just until the egg whites disappear. Spoon the batter into the muffin cups until three-fourths full.

4. Bake for 15 minutes or until golden and set. Let the cakes cool in the pans on racks for 15 minutes, then transfer onto the racks to cool. Sprinkle the tops with confectioners' sugar and top each with a raspberry. These cakes are heavenly when served warm, but they are still delicious when eaten at room temperature.

Baker's Tip: For a delicious Lemon Torte, preheat the oven to 350°F. Butter and flour two 9-inch round layer cake pans and line the bottoms with wax paper. Mix a double recipe of the batter for Lemon Tea Cakes and divide the batter between the pans. Bake for 25 minutes or until a toothpick inserted in the center comes out with moist crumbs. Let the cakes cool in the pans on racks for 15 minutes, then transfer onto the racks to cool. While the cakes cool, make a double recipe of the Cream Cheese Frosting (see frosting for Carrot Cake Cups on page 26). Using a serrated knife, split each layer into 2 thin layers, making a total of 4 layers. Frost between the cooled layers, on the sides, and on top. Refrigerate until ready to serve, then decorate the top with fresh raspberries, if you wish.

Makes 2 1/2 dozen petite lemon tea cakes or one 9-inch four-layer lemon torte.

Cheesecake Bites

These tiny cheesecakes are light, lemony, and oh-so-creamy. For special occasions, I like to pipe a little flower of yellow frosting in the center of each. If you don't happen to be handy with a pastry tube, look for some tiny rosebuds made from frosting in a local cake decorating shop.

Gingersnap Crust
1 1/2 cups gingersnap crumbs (about 8 ounces gingersnaps)
1/2 cup ground blanched almonds
1/2 cup (1 stick) unsalted butter (not margarine), melted

Cheesecake Filling
4 packages (8 ounces each) cream cheese, at room temperature

1 cup granulated sugar
3 large eggs
1 tablespoon vanilla extract
2 teaspoons grated lemon peel

Sour Cream Topping
1 cup dairy sour cream
1 tablespoon sugar
2 teaspoons vanilla extract

1. *To make the Gingersnap Crust:* Line 36 mini-muffin cups (2 inches in diameter, 1 inch deep) with paper liners. In a medium-size bowl, toss together all of the crust ingredients. Press into the bottom and partially up the sides of the paper liners.

2. *To make the Cheesecake Filling:* Preheat the oven to 350°F. In a large bowl, with an electric mixer on high, beat the cream cheese with the sugar until smooth and fluffy. Beat in the eggs, one at a time, then the vanilla and lemon peel. Continue beating 5 minutes more or until light and creamy, scraping the sides of the bowl occasionally.

3. Spoon the batter into the muffin cups until almost full. Bake for 15 minutes or until set in the center. Remove the cakes from the oven (leaving the oven on) and cool the cakes in the pans on racks for 10 minutes.

4. *To make the Sour Cream Topping:* While the cakes cool, mix all of the topping ingredients in a small bowl. Spread on top of the cakes, then return the cakes to the oven and bake 5 minutes more or just until the topping is set. Let the cakes cool in the pans on racks for 30 minutes, then remove to plates, cover, and refrigerate for at least 4 hours.

Baker's Tip: For an impressive large cheesecake, preheat the oven to 350°F. Line the bottom and halfway up the sides of a 9- or 10-inch springform pan with one recipe of the Gingersnap Crust for Cheesecake Bites, then fill with one recipe of the Cheesecake Filling. Bake for 1 hour or until set. Meanwhile make one recipe of the Sour Cream Topping and bake as directed.

Makes 3 dozen mini cheesecake bites or one 9- or 10-inch cheesecake.

Blueberry Gem Jams

In Victorian days, gems were popular childhood treats. Small and scrumptious, they were baked in heavy cast-iron gem pans with rounded bottoms, very much like our popover pans today. Typical of the gem cakes of yesteryear, these have the nutty addition of whole wheat flour—plus we've added fresh blueberries too. Then we've baked them in mini-muffin cups for smaller taste treats.

1 1/2 cups sifted all-purpose flour	1 1/4 cups granulated sugar
1/2 cup sifted whole-wheat flour	2 large eggs
1 tablespoon baking powder	1 pint fresh ripe blueberries, stemmed, washed, and drained (about 2 cups)
1 teaspoon ground nutmeg	
1/2 teaspoon salt	1 cup whole milk
1/2 cup (1 stick) unsalted butter (not margarine), at room temperature	1/2 cup finely chopped blanched almonds

1. Preheat the oven to 350°F. Line 36 mini-muffin cups with paper liners. Onto a piece of wax paper, sift together both of the flours, the baking powder, nutmeg, and salt.

2. In a large bowl, with an electric mixer on high, cream the butter and 1 cup of the sugar until light yellow. Beat in the eggs, one at a time, and continue beating 3 minutes more or until light and fluffy.

3. In a small bowl, mash ¾ cup of the blueberries and blend into the butter mixture. Using a wooden spoon, beat in the flour mixture, one-third at a time, alternating with the milk, beginning and ending with the flour. Gently fold in the remaining 1 ¼ cups of whole blueberries.

4. Fill the cups almost full with the batter, then sprinkle with the almonds and the remaining ¼ cup of sugar. Bake for 15 minutes for mini gem cakes or until a toothpick inserted in the center comes out with moist crumbs. Serve hot!

Baker's Tip: For regular-size blueberry muffins, preheat the oven to 350°F and line 24 regular-size muffin cups with paper liners. Mix one recipe of batter for Blueberry Gem Jams and spoon the batter into the cups until almost full. Bake for 25 minutes or until a toothpick inserted in the center comes out with moist crumbs.

Makes 3 dozen tiny gem jam cakes or 2 dozen regular-size blueberry muffins.

Carrot Cake Cups

"Eat your vegetables" takes on a whole new meaning when the vegetables, in this case carrots, are baked into tiny cake bites. Serve these petite carrot cakes hot from the oven, or cool them and ice with lemony Cream Cheese Frosting. This recipe bakes up perfectly into a large bundt cake too.

Carrot Cakes
2   cups sifted all-purpose flour
2   teaspoons baking powder
2   teaspoons pumpkin pie spice
$1/2$ teaspoon salt
2   large eggs
$1^1/2$ cups granulated sugar
1   cup vegetable oil
1   cup cooked carrot purée (about 3 large cooked peeled carrots)
1   tablespoon vanilla extract
1   cup golden raisins

$1/2$ cup cinnamon applesauce (from the jar)
1   cup finely chopped walnuts

Cream Cheese Frosting
3   packages cream cheese, at room temperature (4 ounces each)
6   tablespoons ($3/4$ stick) unsalted butter (not margarine), at room temperature
$4^1/2$ cups sifted confectioners' sugar (one 1-pound box)
2   teaspoons grated lemon peel

1. *To make the Carrot Cake Cups:* Preheat the oven to 350°F. Line 48 mini-muffin cups (2 inches in diameter, 1 inch deep) with paper liners. Onto a piece of wax paper, sift the flour, baking powder, pumpkin pie spice, and salt.

2. In a large bowl, with an electric mixer on high, beat the eggs and granulated sugar until light yellow. Beating constantly, slowly add the oil, taking 4 or 5 minutes to blend well. Beat in the carrot purée and vanilla.

3. Using a wooden spoon, stir in the flour mixture just until it disappears, then fold in the raisins, applesauce, and walnuts. Spoon the batter into the muffin cups until almost full.

4. Bake for 15 minutes or until a toothpick inserted in the center comes out with moist crumbs. Let the cakes cool in the pans on racks for 5 minutes before turning out onto the racks to cool completely. Frost with Cream Cheese Frosting.

5. *While the cakes cool, make the Cream Cheese Frosting:* In a medium-size bowl, with an electric mixer on high, beat the cream cheese and butter until smooth and fluffy. Reduce the speed to low and slowly blend in the confectioners' sugar and lemon peel. Increase the speed to high and beat until fluffy. Swirl on the top of the cooled cakes.

Baker's Tip: For an impressive bundt cake, preheat the oven to 350°F. Butter and flour a 10-inch bundt cake pan. Make one recipe of batter for Carrot Cake Cups, spoon into the pan, and bake for 1 hour and 10 minutes or until a cake tester inserted in the center comes out with moist crumbs. Cool the cake in the pan on a rack for 15 minutes, then turn out onto the rack to cool. After the cake has cooled completely, frost with one recipe of the Cream Cheese Frosting.

Makes about 4 dozen mini carrot cake cups or one 10-inch bundt cake.

Frosted Fudge Fingers

Almost everyone loves chocolate—at least all of my friends do. And these fudgey fudge cake fingers are one of their favorites. Incidentally, they are mine too, for I can have homemade, frosted chocolate cake in less than an hour—from start to finish!

Fudge Cake Fingers

2 1/4 cups sifted all-purpose flour
2 teaspoons baking powder
1/2 teaspoon baking soda
1/2 teaspoon salt
1 cup (2 sticks) unsalted butter (not margarine), at room temperature
2 cups granulated sugar
3 large eggs
5 squares (1 ounce each) unsweetened chocolate, melted
1 cup chocolate milk
1 tablespoon vanilla extract
1 cup dairy sour cream

Fudge-Nut Frosting

6 tablespoons (3/4 stick) unsalted butter (not margarine)
1/3 cup unsweetened Dutch cocoa powder
7 tablespoons whole milk
4 1/2 cups sifted confectioners' sugar (one 1-pound box)
2 teaspoons vanilla extract
1 cup finely chopped pecans

1. *To make the Fudge Cake Fingers:* Preheat the oven to 400°F. Butter a 15 1/2 × 10 1/2 × 2-inch baking pan and line with parchment or wax paper. Onto a piece of wax paper, sift the flour, baking powder, baking soda, and salt.

2. In a medium-size bowl, cream the butter and granulated sugar until light yellow. Blend in the eggs, one at a time, then the melted chocolate, milk, and vanilla and continue beating 3 minutes more or until light and creamy. Stir in the flour mixture, one-third at a time, alternating with the sour cream, beginning and ending with the flour. Spread the batter evenly in the pan. Bake for 15 minutes or just until the center springs back when it is lightly touched. (Watch closely and do not overbake!)

3. *While the cake bakes, make the Fudge-Nut Frosting:* In a medium-size saucepan, stir the butter, cocoa, and milk over medium heat for 4 minutes or just until the mixture is well blended and begins to bubble. Remove from the heat and quickly stir in the remaining frosting ingredients.

4. As soon as the cake comes out of the oven, gently and evenly spread the frosting with a spatula over the top. Cool the frosted cake in the pan on a rack for at least 1 hour, then cut into 3 × 1 1/2-inch fingers.

Baker's Tip: If there are some leftovers, just pack in self-lock freezer bags and freeze up to a month. (Even the icing freezes beautifully!)

Makes 35 frosted fudge cake fingers.

Dots of Cookies

*Take a look in the cookie jar . . . you'll find lots of
bite-size cookies inside!*

ere are many of your childhood favorites, baked in smaller sizes so you can enjoy them often. Bake up a batch of spicy oatmeal bites . . . pipe out some tiny thumbprint cookies and fill with raspberry jam . . . roll out a galaxy of shining stars for the holidays. Or for any day, mix up a few dozen of that all-time lunch-box favorite of peanut butter cookies, in tiny sizes of course. We've even tucked in a recipe for an old-fashioned refrigerator cookie to slice up and bake. Whichever you choose, be sure to make extras, for they disappear fast!

Ice Cream Cookies

In the days of old-fashioned ice cream parlors, sundaes often arrived with a few cookies on the plate. These little crisp cookies bring back those memories: simple buttery pecan wafers, with just a hint of brown sugar and spice.

1 3/4 cups sifted all-purpose flour
1 teaspoon baking powder
1 teaspoon ground cinnamon
1/2 teaspoon salt
1/2 cup (1 stick) unsalted butter (not margarine), at room temperature
2/3 cup firmly packed light brown sugar

1/2 cup granulated sugar
1 large egg
2 tablespoons heavy cream
1 tablespoon vanilla extract
1 cup finely chopped pecans, toasted

1. On a piece of wax paper, sift the flour, baking powder, cinnamon, and salt. In a large bowl, with an electric mixer on high, cream the butter with both of the sugars until light yellow.

2. Add the egg, then the cream and vanilla, and continue beating until light and fluffy. Using a wooden spoon, stir in the flour mixture just until it disappears. Mix in the pecans.

3. Turn out the dough onto a lightly floured surface and shape it into 2 rolls, 12 × 1 1/2 inches. Wrap each roll of dough tightly in plastic wrap and refrigerate for at least 2 hours or overnight, or up to 1 week. (You may also freeze the rolls of dough for up to 1 month. Just be sure to wrap properly for freezing.)

4. *To bake the cookies:* Preheat the oven to 400°F and butter 4 baking sheets. Using a sharp knife, slice one roll of the chilled or frozen dough 1/4-inch thick. Place cookies 1/2-inch apart on the baking sheets. (Keep the other roll of dough refrigerated or frozen while you're slicing the first batch.)

5. Bake for 8 minutes for chilled dough (10 minutes for frozen dough) or until crisp and lightly browned. Let the cookies stand on the baking sheets on racks for 2 minutes, then transfer with a spatula to the racks to cool. Repeat the slicing and baking of the remaining roll of dough.

Makes about 7 dozen petite ice cream cookies.

Peanut Butter Drops

It seems that my friends, or me either, have ever outgrown our love for peanut butter cookies. These have that extra helping of peanuts in every tiny bite. If you happen to have some cookies left over, place them in a tight-sealing container in the freezer. They freeze perfectly for at least a month.

1 cup all-purpose flour
1/2 teaspoon baking soda
1/2 cup (1 stick) unsalted butter (not margarine), at room temperature
1 cup creamy peanut butter
1/2 cup granulated sugar

1/2 cup firmly packed light brown sugar
1 large egg
3 tablespoons whole milk
1 cup salted peanuts, finely chopped

1. Preheat the oven to 350°F and butter 4 baking sheets. In a small bowl, mix the flour with the baking soda.

2. In a large bowl, with an electric mixer on high, cream the butter and peanut butter with both of the sugars until light brown. Beat in the egg and milk and continue beating until light and fluffy. Using a wooden spoon, stir in the flour mixture just until it disappears, then mix in the peanuts and continue beating until light and fluffy.

3. Drop by rounded teaspoonfuls onto the baking sheets. Using the back of a fork, lightly press the top of each cookie, first in one direction then in the opposite direction, making a crisscross design.

4. Bake for 8 minutes or until light golden brown. Let the cookies cool on the baking sheets on racks for 2 minutes, then transfer with a spatula to the racks to cool.

Makes about 7 dozen peanut butter drops.

Spicy Oatmeal Bites

Oatmeal cookies can often be found in my cookie jar. These have a sugar and spice twist, plus raisins and nuts, that make them even better than most.

1	cup sifted all-purpose flour
1/2	teaspoon baking soda
1/2	teaspoon ground cinnamon
1/4	teaspoon ground nutmeg
1	cup granulated sugar
3/4	cup (1 1/2 sticks) unsalted butter (not margarine), at room temperature

1/3	cup firmly packed light brown sugar
1	large egg
2	teaspoons vanilla extract
1	cup uncooked old-fashioned oats (not instant)
1	cup dark raisins
1	cup finely chopped walnuts

1. Preheat the oven to 350°F and butter 3 baking sheets. Onto a piece of wax paper, sift the flour, baking soda, cinnamon, and nutmeg. On a small plate spread out 1/3 cup of the granulated sugar.

2. In a large bowl, with an electric mixer on high, cream the butter, the remaining 2/3 cup of granulated sugar, and the 1/3 cup brown sugar until light gold. Add the egg and vanilla and continue beating until light and fluffy.

3. Using a wooden spoon, stir in the flour mixture just until it disappears. Mix in the uncooked oats, raisins, and walnuts. Cover with plastic wrap and refrigerate for at least 1 hour or overnight.

4. Dust your hands with a little granulated sugar. Shape the dough into 3/4-inch balls and roll each ball in the granulated sugar on the plate. Place the cookies on the baking sheets, 2 inches apart, and flatten slightly with the palm of your hand.

5. Bake for 15 minutes or just until they start to brown. Let the cookies stand on the baking sheets on racks for 2 minutes, then transfer with a spatula to the racks to cool. These cookies keep for up to a week in an airtight cookie jar or up to a month in the freezer.

Makes about 6 dozen small spicy oatmeal bites.

Raspberry Thumbprints

Cookie-baking day was always fun when I was growing up—and still is! These cookies are ones that are fun to make with children. They love to help make the thumbprint in the center of each.

$2^{1}/_{2}$ cups sifted all-purpose flour
1 teaspoon baking powder
$^{1}/_{2}$ teaspoon salt
1 cup ground blanched almonds
1 cup (2 sticks) unsalted butter (not margarine), at room temperature

$^{2}/_{3}$ cup granulated sugar
5 tablespoons whole milk
1 large egg yolk
1 tablespoon vanilla extract
$^{1}/_{2}$ cup raspberry jam

1. Preheat the oven to 375°F and butter 3 baking sheets. Onto a piece of wax paper, sift the flour, baking powder, and salt, then toss with the almonds.

2. In a medium-size bowl, with an electric mixer on high, cream the butter with the sugar until light yellow; beat in the milk, egg yolk, and vanilla and continue beating until light and fluffy. Using a wooden spoon, stir in the flour mixture.

3. Using a pastry tube fitted with a #8 star tip, pipe into 1-inch rounds onto the baking sheets, about 2 inches apart. (Or drop from a small teaspoon onto the sheets.)

4. Dust your hands with a little flour and make a dent in the center of each cookie with your thumb. Fill the center of each cookie with about $1/4$ teaspoon of jam.

5. Bake for 10 minutes or just until cookies are set and golden. Let the cookies stand on the baking sheets on racks for 2 minutes, then transfer with a spatula to the racks to cool. Store in an airtight container for up to 1 week, but do not freeze. This recipe doubles easily.

Makes about 5 dozen baby thumbprint cookies.

Shining Stars

Welcome to my holiday cookie-making session, where there's a lot of baking going on. These sugar cookies are a "must." For Valentine's Day, I often cut out small hearts from this same dough, then sprinkle the cookies with red colored sugar before baking.

Sugar-Cookie Dough

2   cups all-purpose flour

1 ¹/₂ teaspoons baking powder

¹/₄   teaspoon salt

¹/₄   cup whole milk

1   tablespoon vanilla extract

1   cup (2 sticks) unsalted butter (not margarine), at room temperature

1   cup granulated sugar

2   large whole eggs

1   teaspoon grated lemon peel

Decorations

2   large egg whites

1   tablespoon cold water

    Multicolored decorating sugar

1. *To make the Sugar Cookie Dough:* Onto a piece of wax paper, mix together the flour, baking powder, and salt. Measure out the milk and stir in the vanilla.

2. In a large bowl, with an electric mixer on high, cream the butter and sugar until light yellow. Beat in the 2 whole eggs, one at a time, then the lemon peel, and continue beating until light and fluffy.

3. Stir in the flour mixture, one-third at a time, alternating with the milk mixture, beginning and ending with the flour. Divide the dough into 2 equal pieces, wrap in plastic wrap, and refrigerate for at least 2 hours.

4. Preheat the oven to 350°F and butter 3 baking sheets. On a lightly floured surface, roll out one piece of dough, $1/4$- to $3/8$-inch thick. (Keep the other piece of dough refrigerated while you're rolling out the first batch.) Using a star-shaped cookie cutter about 2 inches in diameter, cut out small stars, dipping the cutter into flour frequently as you go. Using a spatula, transfer the cookies to the baking sheets, and bake for 5 minutes.

5. *While the cookies bake:* Whisk the 2 egg whites in a cup with the water. Lightly brush the cookies with the egg whites and sprinkle with the colored sugar. Bake 2 or 3 minutes more or just until the edges start to brown. Let the cookies stand on the baking sheets for 2 minutes, then transfer to the racks to cool. Repeat with the remaining piece of dough.

Baker's Tip: This dough freezes beautifully. Mix as directed in steps 1–3, wrap for the freezer, and freeze for up to 3 months. Let defrost, then proceed as directed in steps 4 and 5.

Makes about 5 dozen miniature star cookies.

Mini Macaroons

The Italians have been credited with creating the first macaroons from egg whites, almonds, and coconut. But ever since macaroons were introduced in this country by our Italian immigrants, we have been enjoying them, especially at holiday time. In our Texas home, they were always baked at Christmas time, since the weather was cooler, less humid, and thus better for baking them at that time of the year. Now living in New York, I frequently bake them year-round.

3	large egg whites	1	teaspoon vanilla extract
1/4	teaspoon salt	1/2	teaspoon almond extract
3/4	cup granulated sugar	2	cups flaked coconut
1/3	cup ground blanched almonds		

1. Preheat the oven to 350°F and line 3 baking sheets with parchment paper or foil.
2. In a medium-size bowl, with an electric mixer on high, beat the egg whites and salt until frothy. Gradually add the sugar, 2 tablespoons at a time, beating until stiff peaks form. Gently fold in the almonds, then the extracts and coconut.
3. Drop the batter by rounded teaspoonfuls onto the baking sheets. Bake for 10 minutes or just until the cookies begin to brown. Let the cookies stand on the baking sheets on racks for 30 minutes, then peel off the paper and place on the racks to cool completely. Store in airtight containers for up to one week.

Baker's Tip: If you prefer crunchy macaroons, bake as above. Turn off the oven, keeping the door closed, and let the cookies remain in the oven for 15 minutes. Cool as above.

Makes about 6 dozen mini macaroons.

Sugar Balls

Growing up in Texas meant celebrating the Christmas season without snow. But Mom always made these small butterball cookies, then rolled them in powdered sugar. They looked just like little snowballs and quickly became a favorite at every holiday gathering. I still bake these cookies today, often to give to friends we visit on the weekend.

2 1/4 cups sifted cake flour

3/4 teaspoon salt

1 cup (2 sticks) unsalted butter (not margarine), at room temperature

1 1/2 cups sifted confectioners' sugar

1 tablespoon vanilla extract

1 teaspoon almond extract

1 cup finely chopped pecans, toasted

1. Preheat the oven to 325°F and butter 2 baking sheets. Onto a piece of wax paper, sift the flour and salt.

2. In a medium-size bowl, with an electric mixer on high, cream the butter with 3/4 cup of the sugar until light yellow, then beat in the vanilla and almond extracts.

3. Using a wooden spoon, stir in the flour mixture, just until it disappears, then mix in the pecans. Dust your hands with a little of the confectioners' sugar and roll the dough into 1-inch balls.

4. Place the cookies 2 inches apart on the baking sheets and bake for 30 minutes or just until the cookies start to brown. Let the cookies stand on the baking sheets on racks for 2 minutes, then transfer with a spatula to the racks to cool for 15 minutes. Roll in the remaining 3/4 cup of confectioners' sugar. Store in an airtight container for up to 2 weeks, but do not freeze. This recipe doubles easily.

Makes about 4 dozen small sugar balls.

Baby-Bar Cookies

Bake up a batch of baby-bar cookies—
they're homemade and heavenly, bite after bite!

*R*ediscover those old-fashioned bar cookies—the ones that are spread into a pan, then baked all at once . . . no dropping or rolling needed! Some are baked up in a single layer, others in a double deck of shortbread and fruit. Of course, our bar cookies are sliced into baby bars, so you get just as much flavor, but fewer calories in each. Mix up a batch of chocolate chip bars marbled with chocolate . . . stir up some moist cookies from bananas and nuts . . . whip up some light lemon bars for teatime. You'll quickly discover that baby bars are moist and marvelous, as they melt in your mouth at every bite!

Banana Crunch Bars

Mix up a buttery batter, fold in some fresh bananas, then stir in a few butterscotch bits and nuts. You'll have this great cookie that's moist and full of home-baked flavor. They tote great inside a lunch box or picnic basket!

2	cups sifted all-purpose flour		1	cup firmly packed light brown sugar
2	teaspoons baking powder			
1/2	teaspoon baking soda		1/2	cup granulated sugar
1/2	teaspoon salt		2	large eggs
1	cup butterscotch morsels		1/2	cup whole milk
1	cup finely chopped walnuts		1	cup mashed ripe bananas (about 3 medium)
1/2	cup (1 stick) unsalted butter (not margarine), at room temperature			

46

1. Preheat the oven to 350°F and butter a 13 × 9 × 2-inch baking pan. In a medium-size bowl, sift the flour, baking powder, baking soda, and salt, then toss with the butterscotch morsels and walnuts.

2. In a large bowl, using an electric mixer on high, cream the butter with $1/2$ cup of the brown sugar and the granulated sugar until gold. Beat in the eggs, one at a time, then add the milk, and continue beating until light and fluffy. Blend in the bananas. Using a wooden spoon, stir in the flour mixture just until it disappears.

3. Spread the batter in the pan and sprinkle with the remaining $1/2$ cup of brown sugar. Bake for 35 minutes or just until a toothpick inserted in the center comes out almost clean (do not overbake).

4. Transfer the pan to a rack and let the cookies cool completely, then cut into 36 bars, 2 × 1 $1/4$-inches each. Using a narrow spatula, remove the bars from the pan. Store the cookies in an airtight cookie jar, but do not freeze.

Makes 3 dozen mini banana crunch bars.

Mini Marble Bars

Every bake sale and state fair seems to always have at least one display of chocolate chip cookies. This recipe takes those same familiar ingredients, but uses mini chips, of course, instead of the larger ones. As the cookies bake, these little chips melt away, creating marbleized effects of chocolate swirls. They're just bursting with homemade goodness in every bite!

1	cup + 2 tablespoons all-purpose flour	1/2	cup firmly packed light brown sugar
1/2	teaspoon baking soda	1/3	cup granulated sugar
1/2	teaspoon salt	1	large egg
1/3	cup whole milk	9	ounces mini semisweet chocolate chips (1 1/2 cups)
1	tablespoon vanilla extract		
1/2	cup (1 stick) unsalted butter (not margarine), at room temperature	1	cup finely chopped pecans, toasted

1. Preheat the oven to 350°F and butter a 13 × 9 × 2-inch baking pan. Onto a piece of wax paper, mix the flour with the baking soda and salt. Measure out the milk and stir in the vanilla.

2. In a large bowl, with an electric mixer on high, cream the butter with both of the sugars until light gold. Beat in the egg, then the milk mixture, and continue beating until light and fluffy. Using a wooden spoon, stir in the flour mixture just until it disappears, then stir in the chocolate chips and pecans.

3. Evenly spread the batter in the pan and bake for 5 minutes. Run a knife through the batter, creating a marbled effect with the melted chips. Bake 15 minutes more or just until a toothpick inserted in the center comes out almost clean (do not overbake).

4. Transfer the pan to a rack and let the cookies cool completely, then cut into 36 bars, 2 × 1 1/4-inches each. Using a narrow spatula, remove the bars from the pan. Store the cookies in an airtight cookie jar. These cookies stay great in the freezer for up to 1 month.

Makes 3 dozen mini marble bars.

Double-Date Bars

Calling all date lovers! This bar cookie matches up a rich shortbread layer with a date-nut top layer to form an old-fashioned delicious cookie that stays moist, down to the last one. I often bake them for gifts during the holidays.

Shortbread Layer

1 1/2 cups sifted all-purpose flour

3/4 cup (1 1/2 sticks) unsalted butter (not margarine), at room temperature

1/2 cup granulated sugar

1/4 cup water

Date Layer

2/3 cup sifted all-purpose flour

1 teaspoon baking powder

1/2 teaspoon salt

2 cups finely chopped pitted dates

1 cup finely chopped walnuts

3 large eggs

1 1/2 cups firmly packed light brown sugar

1 tablespoon vanilla extract

1/3 cup whole milk

3 tablespoons sifted confectioners' sugar

1. *To make the Shortbread Layer:* Preheat the oven to 350°F and butter and flour a 13 × 9 × 2-inch baking pan. In a medium-size bowl, mix all of the ingredients for the shortbread layer until blended, then press evenly into the bottom of the pan. Bake for 20 minutes or until set but not browned.
2. *To make the Date Layer:* Into a medium-size bowl, sift the flour, baking powder, and salt. Add the dates and walnuts and toss until coated.
3. In a clean medium-size bowl, with an electric mixer on high, beat the eggs until light yellow. Add the brown sugar and vanilla and continue beating until light and fluffy. Using a wooden spoon, stir in the flour-date mixture, one-half at a time, alternating with the milk.
4. Evenly spread the date mixture onto the hot crust, return to the oven, and bake at 350°F for 35 minutes or until the top springs back when lightly touched. If the cookies start to brown too much, lay a piece of foil loosely over the top.
5. Transfer the pan to a rack and let the cookies cool completely. Sprinkle with the confectioners' sugar, then cut into 36 bars, 2 × 1 1/2-inches each. Using a narrow spatula, remove the bars from the pan. Store the cookies in an airtight cookie jar, but do not freeze.

Makes 3 dozen mini double-date bars.

Lemon Lites

Here are some heavenly lemon cream bars, made from a batter that resembles a rich sponge batter, then baked just until golden and cut into thin fingers. They're the perfect complement for a pot of freshly brewed hot tea or even a cooling glass of iced tea on a hot summer's day.

Lemon Bars

1 1/2 cups sifted all-purpose flour
1   teaspoon baking powder
1/2   teaspoon salt
6   tablespoons fresh lemon juice
3   tablespoons water
3/4   cup (1 1/2 sticks) unsalted butter
       (not margarine), at room
       temperature

1 1/4 cups granulated sugar
3   large eggs, separated
1   tablespoon grated lemon peel

Vanilla Cream Frosting

1 1/2 cups sifted confectioners' sugar
1/4   cup heavy cream
1   teaspoon vanilla extract

1. *To make the Lemon Bars:* Preheat the oven to 350°F and butter and flour a 13 × 9 × 2-inch baking pan. Onto a piece of wax paper, sift the flour, baking powder, and salt. In a cup, mix the lemon juice with the water.

2. In a medium-size bowl, with an electric mixer on high, cream the butter with 1 cup of the granulated sugar until light yellow. Add the egg yolks, one at a time, then the lemon peel, and continue beating until light and fluffy. Using a wooden spoon, stir in the flour mixture, one-third at a time, alternating with the lemon juice mixture, beginning and ending with the flour.

3. In a clean medium-size bowl, with the mixer on high, beat the egg whites with clean beaters until soft peaks form. Gradually add the remaining 1/4 cup of granulated sugar and continue beating until stiff. Fold into the batter.

4. Spoon the batter into the pan and bake for 25 minutes or until the center springs back when lightly touched. Transfer the pan to a rack and let the cookies cool completely.

5. *While the cookies cool, make the Vanilla Cream Frosting:* In a small bowl, mix all of the frosting ingredients to make a thin frosting. Drizzle on the top of the cooled cookies. Let set for about an hour, then cut into 36 bars, 2 × 1 1/2-inches each. Using a narrow spatula, remove the bars from the pan. These cookies are best when served within 3 days; store in an airtight container in the refrigerator but do not freeze.

Makes 3 dozen mini lemon bars.

Tiny Tarts

*B*y definition, a tart is a small pie or shell filled with cream, jelly, custard, fruits—or other good things to eat. But our tarts are smaller than most. We've baked them in petite muffin pans, which bake into tiny tarts that give you just two or three bites in each. Each tart begins with a crust that combines the rich flavor of butter with the flaky contributions of a little shortening. Then we've filled them with fresh fruits, custard, or cream, creating tiny tempting pies that are not only divinely delicious, but look luscious too. But be careful; they are so tasty that you might be tempted to eat more than just one!

Tiny Buttery Crusts

Making tender, flaky, and crisp crusts for tiny tarts can be easy, provided you begin with the right recipe. This one mixes in seconds in a food processor. Be sure to follow the processing times to avoid overmixing!

2	cups all-purpose flour	2	tablespoons vegetable shortening
2	tablespoons granulated sugar	1	large egg yolk
1/2	teaspoon salt	3	tablespoons iced water
6	tablespoons (3/4 stick) cold unsalted butter (not margarine)	2	tablespoons fresh lemon juice

1. In the bowl of a food processor, place the flour, sugar, and salt. Process for 1 second to mix thoroughly. Add the butter and shortening and process for 30 seconds or just until the mixture resembles coarse crumbs.

2. Add the egg yolk, water, and lemon juice, then process for about 30 seconds more or until a dough forms. Wrap in plastic wrap, flatten into a 6-inch circle, and refrigerate for at least 45 minutes or overnight.

3. Preheat the oven to 425°F. Line 16 mini-muffin cups with paper liners. Using a rolling pin, roll out the pastry on a lightly floured surface to 1/4-inch thickness. Using a fluted 3-inch round pastry cutter, cut into 16 rounds. Transfer to the muffin cups, pressing the dough on the bottom and up the sides of the cups. Prick the sides and bottoms with the tines of a fork.

4. Bake for 10 minutes or until lightly browned on the edges. For the filling, select one of our recipes that follows, or use one of your favorites.

Baker's Tip: This recipe makes enough dough to form one deep-dish 9- or 10-inch single pie crust.

Makes 16 tiny tart shells or one 10-inch tart shell.

Raspberry Petite Pies

The perfect filling makes perfect tiny tarts. This one starts with either cream cheese or the lighter Neufchâtel cheese, which has one-third less fat and calories. Then the little pies are topped with fresh raspberries. They're fabulous with fresh blueberries too.

1	recipe Tiny Buttery Crusts (page 56)		1	teaspoon granulated unflavored gelatin
1	package (8 ounces) cream cheese		1/2	pint fresh ripe raspberries, washed and hulled (about 1 cup)
1/3	cup granulated sugar		2/3	cup red currant jelly
2	tablespoons fresh lime juice		1	cup heavy cream, whipped
1	teaspoon grated lime peel			Small fresh mint leaves
2	tablespoons water			

1. Mix, shape, bake, and cool the 16 tiny tart shells (see page 56).
2. *While the shells cool, make the cream cheese filling:* In a medium-size bowl, with an electric mixer on high, beat the cream cheese with the sugar until smooth and fluffy. Blend in the lime juice and peel and continue beating for 3 minutes more or until light and creamy, scraping the sides of the bowl occasionally.
3. In a small heat-proof bowl, measure in the water, sprinkle the gelatin over the top, and stir until dissolved. Place the mixture over simmering water until thoroughly melted, then beat quickly into the cheese mixture until completely blended.
4. Spoon this filling into the tart shells until almost full. Top each tart with fresh raspberries, covering the filling completely.
5. *To glaze,* place the currant jelly in a small saucepan and stir over low heat until melted. Spoon about 2 teaspoons of the glaze over the top of each tart. Using a pastry bag fitted with a # 15 star tip or a small spoon, pipe or spoon a whipped-cream star-burst on the top of each tart and garnish with a mint leaf. Refrigerate for at least 30 minutes or until serving time.

Makes 16 petite raspberry pies.

Strawberry Tiny Tarts

Every summer, I simply can't wait until the strawberry fields open on Long Island so I can organize a strawberry picking with my friends. Even the lazy ones come along, for they know this means that fresh strawberry tarts will soon be on the menu!

1	recipe Tiny Buttery Crusts (page 56)		2	large egg yolks
1/2	cup granulated sugar		3	tablespoons unsalted butter (not margarine)
4	teaspoons cornstarch		2	teaspoons vanilla extract
1	teaspoon grated lemon peel		1	pint small whole fresh strawberries, ripe but firm (about 2 cups)
1/2	teaspoon salt		2/3	cup strawberry or red currant jelly
1	cup whole milk			Small fresh mint leaves
1	large egg			

1. Mix, shape, bake, and cool the 16 tiny tart shells (see page 56).
2. *While the shells cool, make the custard filling:* In a medium-size saucepan, mix the sugar, cornstarch, lemon peel, and salt, then whisk in the milk. Cook over medium-high heat, whisking constantly, for 5 minutes or until the mixture comes to a full boil.
3. Meanwhile, in a medium-size bowl, with an electric mixer on high, beat the egg and egg yolks until thick and light yellow. Add about 1 cup of the hot milk mixture, then return all to the saucepan. Cook, whisking constantly, for 5 minutes or until thickened.
4. Remove from the heat and stir in the butter and vanilla. Let cool for 15 minutes. Spoon into the tart shells, filling each almost full, then refrigerate for 30 minutes.
5. Wash and hull the strawberries; set aside the 16 smallest ones, and slice the remaining ones lengthwise. Place one whole berry pointed-end-up in the center of each tart and fan the sliced berries around it, covering the filling completely.
6. *To glaze,* place the currant or strawberry jelly in a small saucepan and stir over low heat until melted. Spoon about 2 teaspoons of the glaze over the top of each tart and garnish with a mint leaf. Refrigerate at least 30 minutes more or until serving time.

Baker's Tip: To make a large tart, shape and bake the pastry in a 10-inch tart pan with a removable bottom. Spoon in all of the filling. Select 3 pints of medium-size strawberries. Use about 16 whole berries, pointed-ends-up, around the outside and 1 large berry in the center. Slice the remaining berries and arrange in circles on the top. Glaze as for the individual tarts.

Makes 16 tiny strawberry tarts or one 10-inch tart.

Lemon Cremes

During one of my trips to England, I discovered lemon curd—a rich buttery-lemony creation that's often spread on fresh scones. Here, I've adapted a variation to fill these tiny tarts.

1	recipe Tiny Buttery Crusts (page 56)	3	large eggs
1/2	cup (1 stick) unsalted butter (not margarine), at room temperature	1	large egg yolk
		1/2	cup fresh lemon juice
		2	tablespoons grated lemon peel
1	cup granulated sugar	1/2	cup heavy cream
1/4	teaspoon salt	1/4	teaspoon ground nutmeg

1. Mix, shape, bake, and cool the 16 tiny tart shells (see page 56).
2. *While the shells cool, make the lemon creme filling:* In a medium-size bowl, with an electric mixer on high, cream the butter, sugar, and salt until light yellow and fluffy. Transfer to a heavy medium-size saucepan or double boiler.
3. In the same bowl, with the mixer on high, beat the eggs and egg yolk until thick and light yellow, then blend in the lemon juice and lemon peel. Fold into the butter mixture in the saucepan.
4. Cook over medium heat, whisking frequently, for 5 minutes or until the mixture becomes a thick, creamy filling. Cool for 20 minutes, then spoon into the tart shells, filling each almost full. Refrigerate for at least 30 minutes or until set.
5. *To decorate:* In a medium-size bowl, whip the cream until stiff peaks form, then blend in the nutmeg. Using a pastry bag fitted with a # 15 star tip or a small spoon, pipe or spoon a scallop of cream around the edge of each tart. Refrigerate at least 30 minutes more or until serving time.

Baker's Tip: To make a large tart, shape and bake the pastry in a 10-inch tart pan with a removable bottom and spoon in all of the filling. Chill until set. Whip 1 cup heavy cream until stiff and flavor with 1/2 teaspoon ground nutmeg, then pipe or spoon on top. Refrigerate for at least 30 minutes more.

Makes 16 tiny lemon cremes or one 10-inch tart.

Petite Pickin's

Petite pickin's are sweet fruit pickin's—
piped, puffed, sauced, or even flamed.

G one are the days when a meal must end with a rich and diet-busting dessert course. Here are the days when a small sweet-something is often more welcomed after a heavy meal than a rich towering cake. Pipe some dessert cheese onto fresh fruit slices . . . fill tiny cream puffs with ripe berries and cream . . . flame dainty dessert crêpes with fresh orange Marnier sauce. Whichever you decide to try, you and your guests will be glad you did!

Fruit Boats

Nothing's more delicious than slices of fresh fruits at their peak of ripeness. To make them party-special, I often pipe them with a sweetened dessert cheese.

³/₄ cup fresh orange juice
4 tablespoons fresh lemon juice
4 assorted ripe fresh fruits, such as apples (Delicious or Granny Smith), peaches, pears, plums
8 ounces dessert cheese, such as L'Explorateur, Brillat-Savarin, or cherry-flavored Gourmandise

1 package (8 ounces) cream cheese, at room temperature
¹/₂ cup sifted confectioners' sugar
¹/₂ cup ground pecans

1. In a large shallow dish, mix the orange juice and 3 tablespoons of the lemon juice. Place a cooling rack on top of a baking sheet.
2. Pick the prettiest fruits you can find—ones at their peak of ripeness, yet still firm. Wash but do not peel them, then core or pit them. Using a serrated fruit knife, cut into slices, 1-inch thick. Immediately place any fruits that tend to brown, such as apples, peaches, and pears, in the juice mixture; let stand about 5 minutes. Transfer all of the fruit slices to the rack, standing them upright, to resemble little boats.
3. In a small bowl, with an electric mixer on medium, beat the dessert cheese and cream cheese until fluffy. Add the sugar and beat just until the sugar disappears. Avoid overbeating, as this might make the cheese too soft to pipe. Stir in the remaining tablespoon of lemon juice.
4. Using a pastry bag fitted with a #18 or #19 open star tip, pipe the cheese lengthwise down the center of each fruit slice. Sprinkle lightly with the pecans, cover with plastic wrap, and refrigerate until serving time.

Baker's Tip: If the cheese becomes too soft to pipe, refrigerate it until cold.

Makes about 3 dozen fruit boats.

Raspberry Cream Puffs

These little puffs begin with a simple buttery pastry mixture called pâte à choux. In French this means "little cabbage-shaped pastry." Coincidentally, that's what the little piped puffs look like as they bake.

Cream Puffs
1	cup sifted all-purpose flour
1	tablespoon granulated sugar
1/4	teaspoon salt
1	cup water
1/2	cup (1 stick) unsalted butter (not margarine)
4	large eggs
1	teaspoon vanilla extract

Raspberry Creme Filling
1	cup heavy cream
3	tablespoons granulated sugar
1	tablespoon vanilla extract
1/2	teaspoon ground cinnamon
1	pint fresh raspberries, hulled, washed, and drained (about 2 cups)
	Fresh small mint leaves

1. *To make the Cream Puffs:* Preheat the oven to 425°F. Line 2 baking sheets with parchment paper or foil. Onto a piece of wax paper, sift the flour, sugar, and salt.

2. In a large saucepan, bring the water and butter to a full boil over high heat, then remove from the heat. Using a wooden spoon, stir in the flour mixture, all at once, and continue stirring vigorously until well blended.

3. Return to medium heat and cook, stirring constantly, for 5 minutes or until the mixture forms a thick ball of dough and the water has evaporated.

4. Remove from the heat and let cool for 5 minutes. With a mixer on medium-high, beat in the eggs, one at a time, beating well after each until the mixture looks smooth again. Beat in the vanilla.

5. Using a pastry bag fitted with a #5B or #6B giant star tip or a small spoon, pipe or spoon the dough onto the baking sheets into about 18 circles, 2 1/2 inches in diameter and 2 inches high. Bake for 20 minutes, reduce the oven temperature to 375°F, and bake 5 minutes more or until the cream puffs are golden and puffed. Turn off the oven.

6. Using a sharp pointed knife, make a small slit in the side of each cream puff to let out the steam, then return the puffs to the still-warm oven for 10 minutes more to dry them out. Let the puffs cool completely, then fill them right before serving.

7. *While the puffs cool, make the Raspberry Creme Filling:* In a small bowl, with an electric mixer on high, beat the cream until frothy, then add the sugar, vanilla, and cinnamon and beat until stiff. Using a serrated knife, split the cream puffs crosswise. Fill and top with the whipped cream and berries, then garnish each with a mint leaf. These are their best when made and served the same day.

Makes about 1 1/2 dozen tiny cream puffs.

Petite Éclairs

These petite pastry logs are made from the same pâte à choux pastry as the cream puffs, then they're filled with a rich custard cream and glazed with a chocolate icing. A scrumptious petite treat!

1   recipe Cream Puffs (see page 68)

Vanilla Custard Filling
1/2   cup granulated sugar
1/4   cup all-purpose flour
2   tablespoons cornstarch
1/2   teaspoon salt
2   cups whole milk
2   large egg yolks
3   tablespoons unsalted butter
    (not margarine)
1   tablespoon vanilla extract

Chocolate Glaze Icing
6   ounces regular-size semisweet
    chocolate chips (1 cup)
1/4   cup heavy cream
1   teaspoon vanilla extract
    Dash salt

1. *To make the éclairs:* Preheat the oven to 425°F. Line 2 baking sheets with parchment paper or foil. Prepare the dough as for Cream Puffs on page 68. Using a pastry bag fitted with a #1D straight ribbon tip or a small spoon, pipe or spoon the dough onto the baking sheets into cylinder strips, about 4 inches long, 3/4 inch wide, and 1 inch high. Bake the éclairs, split them lengthwise, and dry them out in the still-warm oven for 10 minutes as for cream puffs. Let the éclairs cool completely, then fill them right before serving.

2. *While the éclairs cool, make the Vanilla Custard Filling:* In a large saucepan, mix the sugar, flour, cornstarch, and salt. Whisk in the milk until smooth. Bring to a boil, whisking constantly over medium-high heat, and cook for 2 minutes.

3. In a medium-size bowl, with an electric mixer on high, beat the egg yolks until light yellow. Beat about 1 cup of the hot milk mixture into the yolks, then return the yolk mixture to the saucepan. Stir over medium heat for 3 minutes or until the custard thickens. Remove from the heat and stir in the butter and vanilla. Let the custard cool for 15 minutes, then refrigerate until it's time to fill the éclairs.

4. *Just before serving, make the Chocolate Glaze Icing:* In a small saucepan, stir the chocolate chips over medium-low heat until melted; stir in the remaining ingredients. Split the cooled éclairs lengthwise and fill each with about 3 tablespoons of the custard. Drizzle some icing on the top in a zigzag design. Serve immediately!

Makes about 2 dozen petite éclairs.

Orange Marnier Crêpes

Here's my most favorite dessert for a dinner party, for it never fails to impress my guests. Make the batter ahead, for it cooks and tastes even better when it has chilled for at least an hour. For the sauce, choose a fine orange liqueur, then look for some of the largest, sweetest oranges you can find.

Crêpes

3/4   cup sifted cake flour

2   tablespoons granulated sugar

     Dash salt

2   large eggs

1/3   cup whole milk

1/3   cup cold water

1/4   cup (1/2 stick) unsalted butter (not margarine), melted

Orange Marnier Sauce

1 1/2   cups fresh orange juice

2   tablespoons cornstarch

1   tablespoon grated orange peel

6   tablespoons (3/4 stick) unsalted butter (not margarine), at room temperature

2   to 3 tablespoons orange liqueur, such as Grand Marnier, Cointreau, or Triple Sec

3   large oranges, peeled, sectioned, and seeded

1. *To make the crêpe batter:* Into the bowl of a food processor or blender, measure all of the seven crêpe ingredients in the order listed. Process for 30 seconds or until the batter is smooth and slightly thick, scraping the sides of the bowl often. Pour the batter into a pitcher, cover, and refrigerate for 1 to 2 hours.

2. *To cook the crêpes:* Heat a crêpe pan or other shallow skillet (preferably a nonstick one) over high heat. Brush lightly with a little additional melted butter and pour in about 2 tablespoons of batter, tilting it in all directions to evenly spread the batter into 4-inch crêpes.

3. Let each crêpe cook for about 30 seconds on the first side, then about 15 seconds on the second or just until golden and lightly browned. Place on a rack and cover with foil to keep warm. Continue until all the batter is used; you will probably have about 16 crêpes. (The cooked crêpes freeze beautifully!)

4. *Just before dessert time, make the Orange Marnier Sauce:* In a small bowl, whisk the orange juice, cornstarch, and orange peel until blended. In a large chafing dish or flat serving skillet, melt the butter over high heat. Whisk in the orange juice mixture and cook until the sauce thickens. Whisk in the liqueur, then remove from the heat.

5. Place each crêpe in the sauce, turning to coat both sides. Fold each crêpe once in half, then in half again, making small triangles. Cook for about 3 minutes or until heated through. For a dramatic presentation, pour a little extra liqueur in a long-handled spoon, stand aside, and ignite with a long-handled match. Spoon over the flames until they burn out. Serve the crêpes on dessert plates, spoon over a little sauce, and top with a few orange sections.

Makes about 16 little crêpes.

Visions of Sugarplums

And . . . visions of sugarplums
danced in their heads!

Christmas Eve has always been (and still is!) one of the most cherished days of the year. While growing up, we would attend candlelight service at church, come back home, and set out cookies and milk for Santa, then drift off to dreamland as Mom read us *The Night before Christmas.* My dreams seemed to be filled with visions of sugarplums, presents, and all good things on those nights. Ever since, I've often called some of my sweetest creations *sugarplums.* Here I've collected a few—from chocolate-dipped berries to small bites of praline sweetmeats.

These triple-dipped berries are simple—and simply divine! Look for red-ripe berries which are juicy, yet still firm. And buy good confectionery grades of bittersweet and white chocolate, which are often found in gourmet food or cookery shops.

24	large whole fresh ripe straw-berries (with no soft spots)	6	tablespoons (³/4 stick) unsweet-ened butter (not margarine)
12	ounces bittersweet chocolate	6	ounces white chocolate
		1	cup ground blanched almonds

1. Rinse the berries but do not hull them. Dry them well with paper towels.

2. In a heavy medium-size saucepan, melt the bittersweet chocolate with 4 table-spoons of the butter over medium heat, stirring occasionally. Remove from the heat. Working quickly, dip each berry about three-quarters of the way down into the chocolate mixture, then place on a rack to cool for about 30 minutes or until set.

3. Spread the almonds on a plate. In a small saucepan, melt the white chocolate with the remaining 2 tablespoons of butter. Dip the pointed end of each chocolate-coated berry about half-way down into the white chocolate. Then dip the tip of the berry into the almonds. Place on the rack to cool.

Baker's Tip: If either of the chocolate mixtures begins to harden before you have finished dipping, just reheat the mixture with 1 or 2 teaspoons of extra butter.

Makes 2 dozen triple-dipped berries.

Apricot Bourbon Balls

In the South, tiny bourbon balls appear on almost every holiday buffet. This recipe, which I created for my own tree-trimming parties, has a hint of chocolate, in addition to the other traditional ingredients. Make them a few days before you plan to serve them, as their flavors mellow upon standing. If you wish to make them without bourbon, use fresh orange juice instead.

6 ounces regular-size semisweet chocolate chips (1 cup)	2 1/2 cups vanilla-wafer crumbs (about 5 dozen wafers)
1 cup sifted confectioners' sugar	1 1/2 cups finely chopped dried apricots
1/4 cup light corn syrup	1 cup finely chopped pecans
1/2 cup bourbon or fresh orange juice	1 cup granulated sugar

1. In a large saucepan, melt the chocolate chips over low heat. Stir in the confectioners' sugar, corn syrup, and bourbon and bring just to a simmer. Remove from the heat.
2. Stir in the wafer crumbs, apricots, and pecans until well blended. Spread the granulated sugar on a plate and dust a little on your hands. Shape the mixture into 1-inch balls and roll each in the sugar.
3. Store in an airtight container for up to 2 weeks, but do not freeze. For extra flavor, sprinkle a piece of cheesecloth with a little bourbon and lay on top of the bourbon balls in the container.

Makes about 6 dozen bourbon-ball sugarplums.

Petite Pralines

New Orleans will always be one of my most favorite cities. It seems that almost every restaurant and candy store features their own special praline—and I probably have tasted them all! This recipe is for the type I like best: creamy with lots of pecans, sweet enough, rich but not too rich, and flavored with a sprinkling of cinnamon.

2	cups firmly packed light brown sugar	3	tablespoons unsalted butter (not margarine), at room temperature
1	cup granulated sugar	2	teaspoons vanilla extract
1	cup heavy cream	3	cups finely chopped pecans
1	cup water		
1/2	teaspoon ground cinnamon		

1. In a heavy 3-quart saucepan, mix both of the sugars with the cream, water, and cinnamon. Stir constantly over medium heat until the sugars melt. While the sugars melt, occasionally wash any sugar crystals away from the sides of the pan with a damp pastry brush.
2. Continue cooking for about 20 minutes, stirring and washing down the sides of the pan occasionally, until the mixture reaches the soft-ball stage of 238°F. Watch carefully! The temperature rises fast near the end of the cooking time.
3. Stir in the butter, vanilla, and pecans, then continue stirring until the butter melts. Remove from the heat and beat the candy with a wooden spoon for 5 minutes.
4. Drop by teaspoonfuls onto parchment or wax paper, adding 1 teaspoon of boiling water whenever the mixture becomes too thick to drop. Let the pralines cool completely before peeling the candies off the paper. Store in an airtight container in the refrigerator. They freeze beautifully for up to 1 month.

Baker's Tip: When making candies, such as these pralines, even one tiny sugar crystal that fails to dissolve in the syrup can cause a chain reaction called "seeding," making the whole batch grainy. So, it's very important that you continuously wash away any sugar crystals that form on the sides of the pan while the candy cooks. Your pralines will come out smooth and glossy—not grainy.

Makes about 8 dozen petite pralines.

Everyone, well almost everyone, loves
chocolate—the richer the better!

It all began well before the colonists arrived: the Aztec Indians were pounding cocoa beans, mixing them with water (with no sweeteners!), and calling it *xocolatl*, or "bitter water." They prized it dearly, for they truly believed it was food from the gods. The Spanish added the sweetening of sugar—and the chocolate craze began. Today, chocolate delights the young, the old, and everyone in-between. I've collected some of my most prized chocolate creations here, then made them in small sizes, of course. As many of my friends say as they taste them: "It's no wonder we all love chocolate!"

Little Chip Cookie Kisses

The now-famous Toll House cookie was created by Mrs. Wakefield at the Toll House Inn in Whitman, Massachusetts, by adding small bits of chocolate to the batter of a popular American cookie called the Butter Drop-Do. Naturally, our recipe uses the little chocolate chips, along with some of the regular-size ones too, to form tiny kisses of the chocolate chip cookie.

1	cup all-purpose flour	1	tablespoon vanilla extract
1/2	teaspoon baking soda	1/2	teaspoon hot water
1/2	teaspoon salt	6	ounces regular-size semisweet chocolate chips (1 cup)
1/2	cup (1 stick) unsalted butter (not margarine), at room temperature	3	ounces mini semisweet chocolate chips (1/2 cup)
6	tablespoons granulated sugar	1	cup finely chopped pecans, toasted
6	tablespoons firmly packed light brown sugar		
1	large egg		

1. Preheat the oven to 375°F and butter 3 baking sheets or line them with parchment paper. Onto a piece of wax paper, sift together the flour, baking soda, and salt.
2. In a large bowl, with an electric mixer on high, cream the butter with both of the sugars until light yellow. Add the egg, then the vanilla and water, beating for 3 minutes or until creamy and fluffy. Using a wooden spoon, stir in the flour mixture just until it disappears, then fold in all of the chocolate chips and pecans.
3. Drop by rounded teaspoonfuls, 2 inches apart, onto the baking sheets. Bake for 10 minutes or just until light brown. Let the cookies cool on the baking sheets for 2 minutes, then transfer with a narrow spatula to a wire rack to cool. Store in an airtight container for up to 2 weeks or in the freezer for up to 1 month. This recipe doubles easily.

Baker's Tip: Freeze cookies as fresh as possible, preferably the day you bake them. Be sure to let them cool completely before wrapping them for the freezer. (The freezer-lock bags work great, especially for cookies!)

Makes about 6 dozen little cookie kisses.

Choco-Toffee Turtles

While growing up in Texas, my friends and I often treated ourselves to a trip to the local sweet shop, where we could usually see fresh turtles being made. They were chunky bites of chocolate, nuts, and caramels, which I loved! I've taken those same flavors and dropped them into a cookie batter to make these choco-toffee wonders.

2   cups sifted all-purpose flour

1/2   teaspoon baking soda

1/2   teaspoon salt

3/4   cup (1 1/2 sticks) unsalted butter (not margarine), at room temperature

2/3   cup granulated sugar

1   large egg

4   squares (1 ounce each) semisweet or bittersweet chocolate, melted and cooled

1/3   cup butterscotch caramel fudge topping (often found near the ice cream freezer in your grocery store)

1   tablespoon vanilla extract

1   cup finely chopped pecans, toasted

1. Preheat the oven to 375°F and butter 3 baking sheets or line them with parchment paper. Onto a piece of wax paper, sift together the flour, baking soda, and salt.
2. In a large bowl, with an electric mixer on high, beat the butter with the sugar until light yellow. Add the egg, the cooled melted chocolate, butterscotch caramel fudge topping, and vanilla, then continue beating for 3 minutes or until light and fluffy. Using a wooden spoon, stir in the flour mixture just until it disappears, then fold in the pecans.
3. Drop by teaspoonfuls, 2 inches apart, onto the baking sheets. Bake for 10 minutes or just until light brown. Let the cookies cool on the baking sheets on racks for 2 minutes, then transfer with a narrow spatula to the racks to cool. Store in an air-tight container for up to 2 weeks or in the freezer for up to 1 month. This recipe doubles easily.

Baker's Tip: If you are unable to find the butterscotch caramel fudge topping, just plain butterscotch topping works fine too.

Makes about 6 dozen tiny choco-toffee turtles.

Baby Brownies

What's a brownie? It's not exactly a cake, nor a cookie—but a delicious combination of both. And it has been an American favorite ever since its creation in the late 19th century. This one has the same rich brown color (hence its name of brownie), plus three kinds of chocolate, giving even more fudgey flavor than most. And naturally, we've cut them into baby sizes.

1	cup (2 sticks) unsalted butter (not margarine)	1	teaspoon salt
3	squares (1 ounce each) unsweet-ened chocolate	2	cups finely chopped walnuts
		4	large eggs
2	squares (1 ounce each) semisweet or bittersweet chocolate	2	cups granulated sugar
		1	tablespoon vanilla extract
1 1/2	cups sifted all-purpose flour	3	ounces mini semisweet chocolate chips (1/2 cup)

1. Preheat the oven to 325°F and butter a 13 × 9 × 2-inch baking pan or two 9-inch square pans. In a small saucepan, melt the butter with the two types of chocolate over low heat, then cool. Onto a piece of wax paper, sift the flour and salt, then toss with the walnuts.

2. In a large bowl, with an electric mixer on high, beat the eggs until frothy. Add the sugar, then the cooled chocolate mixture and the vanilla, beating just until blended.

3. Stir in the flour mixture just until it disappears, then fold in the chocolate chips. Spoon the batter into the pan and bake for 35 minutes or just until a toothpick inserted in the center comes out almost clean. (Do not overbake!)

4. Let the brownies cool in the pan on a rack for 15 minutes then cut into 36 bars, 2 × 1 1/4 inches each. Transfer the brownies with a narrow spatula to the racks to cool. Store in an airtight cookie jar. These brownies freeze great for up to 1 month.

Baker's Tip: When mixing the batter for these brownies and other cookies, be sure to stir in the flour mixture "by hand" with a wooden spoon. Avoid using the electric mixer for this step. Your cookies will be more tender and delicious!

Makes 3 dozen baby brownies.

Tiny Tempting Truffles

It seems that every candy shop has discovered truffles—in every flavor combination imaginable. I still prefer these simple ones: deep, dark, and rich in chocolate flavor, with just a hint of coffee, and rolled in a fine dusting of Dutch cocoa.

3/4 cup heavy cream

6 tablespoons granulated sugar

2 teaspoons instant coffee powder or granules (undiluted)

12 ounces bittersweet chocolate, chopped

1/4 cup (1/2 stick) unsalted butter (not margarine)

1/2 cup sifted Dutch cocoa powder

1. In a heavy 3-quart saucepan, heat the cream, sugar, and coffee powder over medium heat just until bubbles begin to form around the outside edge. Reduce the heat to medium-low and simmer, stirring frequently, for 10 minutes.

2. Stir in the chocolate and butter and continue to cook until both have completely melted. Pour into a shallow, freezer-proof dish. Cover and freeze for at least 1 hour or until firm, yet still moldable.

3. Using a melon baller or teaspoon, shape into 1-inch balls and place on a tray lined with parchment or wax paper. Cover with plastic wrap, then return to the freezer for 1 hour more or until firm.

4. Onto a piece of wax paper, spread out the cocoa powder, then roll the truffles in the cocoa to coat. If there are any truffles left, store them in the freezer for up to 1 month. Be sure to let them thaw before serving.

Makes about 4 dozen tiny tempting truffles.

Love-Me-Forever Fudge

Whether it's Valentine's Day or not, this fudge is guaranteed to bring loving smiles from your sweetheart—and others too!

1/4 cup (1/2 stick) unsalted butter (not margarine)

1 cup heavy cream

2 1/4 cups granulated sugar

1/4 pound mini marshmallows (about 2 1/2 cups)

1 ounce bittersweet or unsweetened chocolate, chopped

6 ounces semisweet chocolate chips (1 cup)

6 ounces sweet milk chocolate

1 tablespoon vanilla extract

2 cups finely chopped pecans

1. Butter a 9-inch square pan or heat-proof dish. In a large, heavy saucepan, stir the butter, cream, and sugar over medium-high heat until the mixture comes to a boil. Lower the heat, cover, and simmer for 5 minutes (without stirring).

2. Stir in the marshmallows and all of the chocolates until melted and smooth. Remove from the heat and stir in the vanilla and pecans.

3. Pour into the pan, let the candy cool on a rack for 30 minutes, then refrigerate for about 2 hours or until firm. Cut into 36 squares, 1 1/2 × 1 1/2 inches each.

Makes 3 dozen petite fudge squares.

Index

International Conversion Chart

These are not exact equivalents: they've been slightly rounded to make measuring easier.

LIQUID MEASUREMENTS

American	Imperial	Metric	Australian
2 tablespoons (1 oz.)	1 fl. oz.	30 ml	1 tablespoon
1/4 cup (2 oz.)	2 fl. oz.	60 ml	2 tablespoons
1/3 cup (3 oz.)	3 fl. oz.	80 ml	1/4 cup
1/2 cup (4 oz.)	4 fl. oz.	125 ml	1/3 cup
2/3 cup (5 oz.)	5 fl. oz.	165 ml	1/2 cup
3/4 cup (6 oz.)	6 fl. oz.	185 ml	2/3 cup
1 cup (8 oz.)	8 fl. oz.	250 ml	3/4 cup

SPOON MEASUREMENTS

American	Metric
1/4 teaspoon	1 ml
1/2 teaspoon	2 ml
1 teaspoon	5 ml
1 tablespoon	15 ml

WEIGHTS

US/UK	Metric
1 oz.	30 grams (g)
2 oz.	60 g
4 oz. (1/4 lb)	125 g
5 oz. (1/3 lb)	155 g
6 oz.	185 g
7 oz.	220 g
8 oz. (1/2 lb)	250 g
10 oz.	315 g
12 oz. (3/4 lb)	375 g
14 oz.	440 g
16 oz. (1 lb)	500 g
2 lbs	1 kg

OVEN TEMPERATURES

Farenheit	Centigrade	Gas
250	120	1/2
300	150	2
325	160	3
350	180	4
375	190	5
400	200	6
450	230	8